SO MUCH SKY

So Much Sky

Jan Willem Schulte Nordholt

Translated by

Henrietta Ten Harmsel

with a foreword by

Frederick Buechner

William B. Eerdmans Publishing Company
Grand Rapids, Michigan

255 Jefferson Ave. S.E., Grand Rapids, Michigan 49503

Translated from the Dutch by arrangement with J. W. Schulte Nordholt
and Uitgeverij de Prom, Baarn, the Netherlands
Printed in the United States of America

00 99 98 97 96 95 94 7 6 5 4 3 2 1

ISBN 0-8028-0831-X

A few of the translations in this volume have previously appeared in *Dialogue,* Calvin College, *The Banner, The Reformed Journal,* and *Perspectives,* all of Grand Rapids, Michigan, and in *The Cresset,* Valparaiso University, Valparaiso, Indiana.

Contents

Foreword

Jan Willem Schulte Nordholt, hitherto known in this country primarily as a scholar, teacher, and historian of international reputation, is revealed in this volume as a poet and photographer of rare spiritual insight. One of the most haunting of his photographs is the one that accompanies the poem "River." In the foreground is a broad expanse of water which looks less like a river than like a shallowly flooded lowland of some kind reflecting the grey sky. The faintly rippled surface is broken here and there by thickets of partly submerged brush and shrubbery. On the far side of the water, in one long horizontal sweep, there is a distant town with only a scattering of rooftops visible, a row of slender trees on the horizon, a church with a spire. The upper half of the picture consists entirely of the immense and overcast sky with a few bands of pale sunlight fanning earthward through a break in the clouds. There is the barest suggestion of gathering storm about it — or is it the first silvery return of fair weather? — but more than anything else the photograph has a mother-of-pearl, translucent quality of deep stillness about it which somehow both rests the eyes and at the same time invites them to look farther and deeper, which calms and at the same time faintly troubles the reflecting spirit, stirs it up. The poem tells us that the water is a snowy sheet, a white bird's wing, a bridal veil, hiding the death and the darkness of things, but that nonetheless darkness is still there. The final couplet catches us by surprise then with yet another "nonetheless," which is that ultimately death is the great healer and that the deepest darkness is precisely that over which the Holy Ghost broods, as in the opening lines of Genesis, bringing about new light, new life, the creation itself.

"River" suggests much about other poems in this collection, which, like the photograph, offer a kind of spiritual rest or benediction but also invite us to look farther and deeper. They are poems of faith in the double sense of being in many cases both about faith and also the products of the faith of the poet himself. "Childlike, I pedal down each unknown lane, / straight and contented, never knowing why / God ever chose to give me so much sky" is the way he describes himself in "Polderland," the poem from which the book's title is taken. And at one level the faith that illumines these pages is a childlike one that takes things as they come like the cyclist on his journey and is no more apt to ask hard questions than Blumhardt, presumably some legendary Dutch eccentric in the sonnet that bears his name, who keeps his horse and carriage in perpetual readiness so that when Christ comes again in his glory, he, Blumhardt, will be able to drive to meet him in a proper conveyance and properly attired in his "tall hat and Sunday best." Childlike, too, is much of the language of the poems, or at least the way it comes through in English translation. There is a directness and simplicity about it that fits well with the short, hymn-like stanzas and traditional rhyme schemes. "Surely God will return here in these skies; / this is the landscape for his paradise," the cyclist muses, and the similarly devout and hopeful tone of many more of the poems makes one wonder if they, like the water in the photograph, have perhaps served the poet himself as white wings, bridal veils, a "shining hood," for hiding his own "things of night and darkness."

But Schulte Nordholt is too honest in his faith, too

faithful to the realities of his own experience, to hide such things completely. In the sestet of the Blumhardt sonnet, for instance, he imagines the old Dutchman, who did not live to witness the Second Coming for which he had made such long and elaborate preparations, lying in his grave, and then asks God directly, "What will you do with all of us who wait / in this dark age, longing for your return, / calling to you with pleading, doubtful sound?" It was Paul Tillich who said somewhere that doubt is not the opposite of faith but an element of faith, and it is certainly an element as well of many of these poems — doubt as the shadow that faith casts, the *in spite of* that keeps faith honest and dynamic instead of merely a mark of piety. Maybe especially in the photographs which he has so lovingly taken of the world of the Netherlands — its landscapes and buildings, its bridges, its works of art — the poet again and again gives praise for "so much sky" and all that the sky represents of God's other great gifts to the world; but God as God is always elusive, "a gleam of mist — / a breath of life that's unapproachable," as none knows better than the Apostle Thomas, who is the subject of another of the sonnets. "He is so holy, he does not exist," Thomas says, and then, like a sudden catch of breath, there is a break between that line and the next — "if I can't really touch him with this hand" — during which we are for a breathless moment confronted with doubt in its ultimate form.

More than any other single theme, death is the subject of many of the poems, and these contain some of Schulte Nordholt's most unforgettable images. One of them describes the photograph of a touchingly ingenuous carving of a man and wife shown both lying in their tomb above and also, just below, kneeling side by side with their hands clasped to suggest a love "that lives eternally" ("First Love").

And there are two others ("Ice-skating" and "After Ice-skating"), in the first of which death is seen as the shadows deep within the ice over which the skater glides at sunset with "snow-white winged shoes," and in the second of which the skater on his way home "on wooden feet" sees himself as "a child of death, a small, stiff-walking man, / a Hollander," who is nonetheless comforted with the knowledge that when night comes, he will dream "that on swift-flying feet / I sweep along the heavens like a star, / one moment still a god, and then no more." Faith as a dream too beautiful not to be in love with, doubt and death as realities too devastating either to hide for long or to hide from — they are, to the poems, what light and dark are to the photographs, giving them their luminous depth and humanness.

Not knowing Dutch, I cannot comment intelligently on Henrietta Ten Harmsel's translation, but her credentials are impeccable — she traveled to The Hague to receive the prestigious Martinus Nijhoff Award for translation from the Dutch. And as an old and dear friend of Dr. Schulte Nordholt, she clearly has a feeling not only for the language in which he writes but also for what he has it in his heart to say. The two of them are apparently in agreement that the basic goal in translating poetry is to produce a good poem, and together, it seems to me, this is what they have done. On the surface these are simple poems simply expressed, but like the water that floods the landscape, leaving just a partly submerged shrub here and there to suggest the complexities beneath, or like the ice that the skater glides on over a world of shadow and mystery, they have depths which invite us to explore our own deep places. A poet has perhaps no higher calling.

Frederick Buechner

Polderland

The distance comes to meet me endlessly,
goes through me, drops behind me, then gets lost.
Childlike I pedal down each unknown lane,
straight and contented, never knowing why
God ever chose to give me so much sky,

so many clouds of white, so many dreams
with such endless varieties of gray.
Surely God will return here in these skies;
this is the landscape for his paradise.

The evening falls. If I ride through the dark,
then the great sounds of wind and rain appear —
the only landscape in my inner ear.

River

As if a sheet of snowy white were laid
over the deep deep darkness of a dream
so now the morning light lies on the stream
of this broad river, pearl against the shade

from dike to dike stretched out, a shining hood,
as if a pure white bird spread out its wings
with their majestic breadth to hide the things
of night and darkness, blot them out for good.

Forget tonight, in heaven's name forget
your anguish, all the pains of yesterday;
they now are swallowed up, their history
is overshadowed with a bridal net.

Water of death is that which heals the most;
on deepest darkness broods the Holy Ghost.

The Man below Me

The man who lives below me plays each night
at the same time and always the same song,
on an old organ; soothing, slow, and light
the tones work through to me, and it takes long
after he stops before I start again
with my own work and dreams. I hum the tune
he played — "Abide with me" — and then
I sing, "Life's little day will vanish soon."

Sometimes in some old painting we may see
an angel play an organ joyfully —
imagination of some childlike soul.

If that were true, then I would reach my goal,
rise at your feet to sing spontaneously,
"O Lord, you always did abide with me."

Blumhardt

His coach stood ready all his whole life long
with horses, reins, and robe, in case the time
should be fulfilled in which the angels' song
would ring out gloriously, then he would climb
into his seat — tall hat and Sunday best —
sitting up straight, he would go trotting forth
to meet his Lord, who'd surely come at last —
and now for good — as King of all the earth.

O God, what have you done with such a heart,
so full of homesickness and such great dreams?
He now lies still and waiting in the ground.
What will you do with all of us who wait
in this dark age, longing for your return,
calling to you with pleading, doubtful sound?

Bridge

The bridge lies stretched from town to land
over the water like a hand

which with its fingers spread out wide
holds back the shore on either side.

The welcome which the traveler hears
sounds cool and stubborn to his ears —

both tower and gate are asking for
the password from the traveler.

Only the soft reflection shows
a sign the dubious traveler knows.

Just like a poem, which seems to say
both "Welcome" and yet "Stay away."

Whose ending really forms its start,
uniting while it holds apart —

a watchtower on the river's strand —
a bridge, an open, outstretched hand.

Poem

The birth pangs of a poem by night
may seem inspired and feather light,
shaped easily — but that's a lie,
creating is painful: it makes us cry.

What first seems light soon weighs like lead,
hours pass — the final word not said.
The weary night has almost passed
before the poem comes home at last.

The careful shepherd seeks the word
that fits exactly with his herd;
he seeks the poor and wandering sheep
that he hears bleating in his sleep.

He waits for the first light to come:
the sudden sunrise of his poem.

Drawing a Horse

It should be like the curved neckline
the way it flows into the back;
just what I want — as if a hand
stroked down a neck, both firm and slack.

If I could catch the gleaming gulf —
that bow of light, the sides of plush
with veins spread out along the flanks
like fine-cut branches on a bush.

And then that head in pride held high,
that pointed ear, the round moist eye,
that warm nose and the mouth with foam,

and the broad tail, that sweeping plume;
and then the legs with hoofbeats' sound
that thunder through the trees and ground.

The War Is Not Over

Death knocks at the door just as the Nazis did
because he is so used to winning out;
he does not wait politely for "Come in,"
but crashes through the door into the house.

Of course, no living soul is ever ready
to think of deportation or to go.
There is so much on earth still to be loved,
so much to learn that we still do not know.

But death holds roundups in street after street,
in trainloads full of folks we're carried off,
and nobody shows up to help us out;

no radio says the invasion has begun,
no speedy fighter planes break through the night.
O God, our greatest Ally, quickly come!

Overexposure

No, on the negative this photograph
does not reveal the angel very well;
yes, the garage and also the new car,
and at the right the family dinner bell.

That lady in the lawnchair is my mother,
and at the window, see my brother stand.
He is dead now. Am I my brother's keeper?
It is my lot to meet him in that land.

That is the way with folks, they have to die;
then some will say, now they exist no more,
and others say, now they are with the Lord.

Only on photos sometimes you can see
the dead with the survivors standing there,
but not the angels with them in the air.

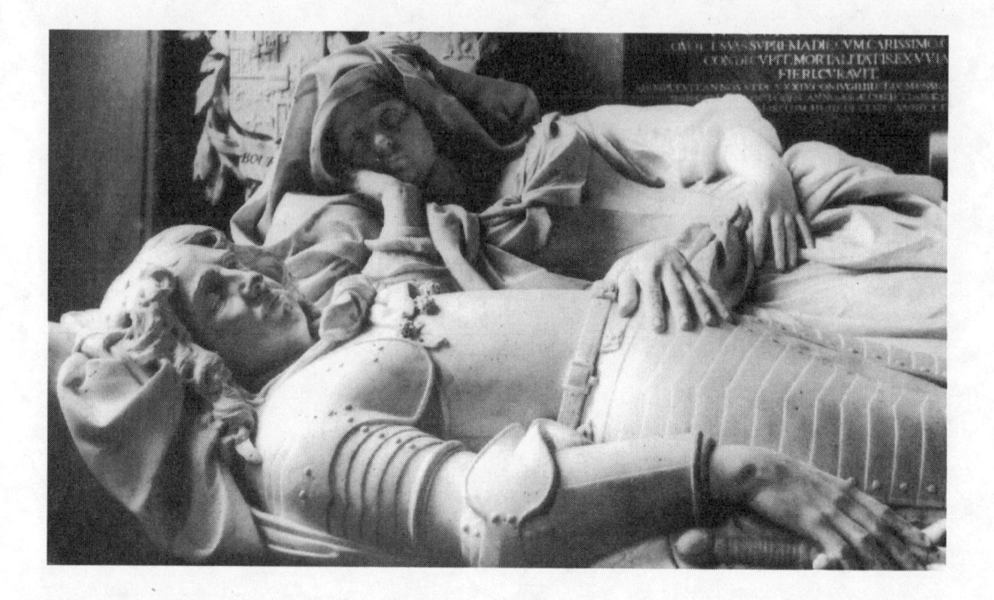

Till Death . . .

How sweet they lie, in silence deep,
a man who only wants to sleep,
a wife who hides what she might feel
and looks askance, with mute appeal
over the man who sleeps like stone,
into blank space, for good alone.
For good her partner stays the same —
a marble man, a marble name.
Translucent stone unites, divides
them now as long as time abides.

Four Heart Poems

Monitor I

Fireflies flicker up in the dark
with restless regularity;
they trace on the screen of twilight,
which stands stretched out for me,
the rhythm of the great heartbeat
of creation.
And thus it will occur
that we will be healed,
slow but sure,
by nature's monitor.

Monitor II

The Alps in a long restless row
pass by along the blackened glass.
As in a mirror, in the dark
we see that nature's riddles pass
quite sensibly — untainted life:
a range of mountains written clear,
each peak shoots up, a shining knife,
suddenly lit by some star's light,
then disappears into the night.

I see in mountains and in dales
how this old earth of ours inhales —
all night, as through an open door,
the microcosm of my monitor.

Heartscript

A restful handwriting fills out for me
the glassy page; it works quite patiently.
It glides along over the smooth black space,
a look of secret pleasure on its face.

A bit too scholarly, so neat and clear,
though now and then a quick peak may appear.
The pen is homesick, teachers used to say;
the space too small, it wants to run away.

The pen is homesick, therefore it takes aim
but cannot slip outside the window's frame.
It is restrained; that may be good for me:
my heart's blood writes my true biography,

ardently writing with one beam of light
my life as if it were a wordless poem
of which the meaning later will strike home.

Mene Tekel

Now everything is different than it was.
My eyes keep following the darkened glass —
that foreign script that slides and glistens by
as silent as a wrinkle in the sky.

I cannot read the language though I know
it tells the history of my heart and soul.
I look away; who knows what may occur?
It frightens me; I feel like Belshazzar.

My life is being weighed, I see it all —
a light-thread dancing on the darkened wall.
And what does doctor Daniel read therein?
Mene mene tekel upharsin.

Little Adam

A brusque and boorish man, walking barefoot,
who with his left hand gives a forceful jerk
to pull the little Jonah from the whale,
awakening little Adam from death's pale;
who saves the human race by hook or crook,
a God like Gulliver in Lilliput.

Psalmrhyming

It all began with David,
who sang sweeter than anyone.
David is dead, for poets
rise and set like the sun.

He always loved life to the fullest:
he played, he danced, he kissed;
he suffered life's deepest sorrows,
now he is lying at rest.

But everywhere on the mountains
around Jerusalem,
everywhere in the world
we hear him singing again.

Everywhere on the organs
he lays his hands on the harp —
in love with his home in the sky —
and always he has his followers:
Vondel, Revius, Gezelle,
Wim Barnard, Jan Wit, and I.

Evangelist

Planting my pen in the heavy earth —
deep earth of true reality —
I plow the world with the clear plowshare
of the Spirit who is guiding me.

Until the time will be fulfilled,
the virgin give birth, her majestic son
go walking through the fields of grain
and hang on the cross until he has borne

all that lay hidden in the fields,
all the horizon's secret pain,
silently buried from any view,

and on the third day rise again.
Everything that my word began
walks with him in the grass and dew.

Knight

In the distance there he rides,
power none would dare defy,
in the sharp-lined silhouette
standing out against the sky;
shining like an ebon star,
casting shadows everywhere,
kingpin, ruler, prince, or czar,
axle of the world up there.

Every riser of the steps
is a line of reckoning,
underlining just how great
is the power of this "king."
How so far-off and so small,
he can be so close and tall.

Dream

I dreamed one night — it seemed like truth —
I was my father in his youth.
I stood in kneepants and hunter's hood
before the house of my flesh and blood.
I did not hear the wind in the trees,
I only saw what a hunter sees.

A lady came through the field of hay,
I kissed her mouth and led her away.
We walked together through the door,
thrilling like birds and wanting more.
But the steps went straight up into the sky,
and the stars clanged out a loud white cry.

When I embraced her, I felt myself fall,
down, down deep, where the waters call.
There on the barren frightened strand
stood all the children, hand in hand.
I heard the crying of the sea,
the wind brought a cold new day to me.

A Jewish Man

A Jew who dates back to the zero year,
who barely reached the age of thirty-three,
then died for our transgressions, back when we
were still living like wild Batavians here.

Yes, stranger still, once he was really dead,
and lay secure and sealed behind a stone,
reported to have risen, big as life,
body and soul, one spring dawn, it is said.

Yes, he was seen and heard and even touched,
and then ascended through a cloud to heaven,
where now he rules for all eternity.

One day he will surprise us like a thief —
who knows, perhaps after a thousand years,
perhaps tonight. He knows the time and day.

regnabo
regno

Fortune's Wheel

This is a poor little jaunty man
who thinks he can change the world,
climbs onto the rim of fortune's wheel,
grasps the structure, gets the feel,
child becomes man, slave becomes king:
"I am the ruler of everything."

He becomes king, sits on his throne;
the wheel keeps circling, nothing goes wrong.
High on the wheel of history
he dreams, "I'm god, just look at me."
He claps his hands, but that is dumb,
for the wheel has other things to come.

Then the revolution turns sore:
"I rule, but I will rule no more!
What good is my scepter to me now?
I'm falling down, my head brought low."
Just see — a body without a soul —
broken; the wheel has taken its toll.

People who follow, look at me:
the glory of life is brief, you see.

About God and Me

I

I draw toward it, I feel it drawing me
just as the grain bows down beneath the freight
of cold, wild snow, and all its golden weight
is darkened and its singing hushed away;

so, overpowered by a matchless might
which like a winter settles down on me,
I draw toward it, I feel it drawing me
to keep the faith throughout the long, long night:

the peace of nature, cold and snowy white,
which breaks all things and makes them black and deep,
the quietness of wisdom and of death.

But I beseech, beseech You, God of fire,
that You remain the voice within my heart,
the unrest which will make my future start.

II

Yes, certainly, I write with my own hand
the wild, chaotic nature of all things,
I lay the measurements of space and time,
I name the names, find the connecting links.

I pull the lines of written history,
I draw the lassos of the sun and moon.
O, world, where I shall someday disappear,
riddle of order, I take charge of you.

And yet, and yet, a moment sometimes comes
that sets me free from all my certainty.
In showers of pity I record each day,
in rapturous sunlight, "Here am I," I say,
"and there are You." What kept apart before,
unites us now: You are my God and Lord.

Lavastone

Even if all the sea, said Jacob Böhm,
were one inkwell, and all the trees together
one great penholder, and the entire earth
one sheet of paper, that were not enough
with which to put God's greatness into words.

And who would hold the pen? That is the question.
Who reads the letter? Does God write to us,
or do we write to him? That cannot be,
for only he can hold that mighty pen
and write God's glory out on nature's page.

He writes himself, it really comes to that;
therefore, it is not readable for us.
For who can really grasp what stands engraved
in nature's book? Who reads the lavastone —
incomprehensible, that runic script?

No matter how we read, research, or dig,
we always read as in a darkened glass
where everything is strange and riddle-like.
The language there is written without words,
the word in there is hidden in the light.

Wintergrove

God holds us tight from age to age,
he never lets his people go.
Just as in a cold wintergrove,
the black, straight trunks rise from the snow

as signs of God's great faithfulness;
the darkness springs from light below,
and in a land of tears and pain
God's covenant sustains its glow.

For everything that God began
he rounds off perfect as a poem.
Look, in the dark horizon's glow
behind the trees, the lights of home.

Existence

Here walks the *I,* trying to find itself,
amazed, it sees the showers and the grass.
It thinks: how blind and aimlessly I walk;
who makes this heart to beat, these steps to pass?
It listens to the streaming of the wind.

Here walks the *I,* it meets itself in alleys,
yet it recalls but slowly where they went.
It sees the houses, long and somber structures,
standing against the hard blue firmament.
So lonesome here, it seems, and left behind.

Here walks the *I,* but where did it start out from,
come to this moment, to this open place,
find itself in this black and secret forest,
here in this moonlit, glowing waterspace,
awake, and still with dreams that fill its mind?

Here walks the stranger *I,* it turns its feet
where to, where to? It does not know the way.
But still *it is.* It wants to greet creation
with a new love and age-old song today.
Here walks the *I;* it's God it wants to meet.

First Love

There we are, those vertical feet
tied fast to our mortality.
Cold and formal we lie atoning
for our earthly, sweet felicity.

Gone by, gone by — so won, so run —
exactly this way we abide;
as we kneel there, so once we began
with our sweet love, side by side.

Wanderer, standing still at our grave,
if our existence appeals to you,
if you read in those soles and skirts
our noble and dignified lives anew,
look at that handclasp, there you see
our love, that lives eternally.

Uneasy with My God

I, too, like Strauss or like the sage Renan
and many more enlightened gentlemen
will analyze the strange phenomenon,
the parables and fables of the one
who walked the field of corn in Canaan.

Historically it can be understood —
the old myth can be clearly heard in it:
a god would want to have a virgin birth,
do wonders, and die off like stalks of wheat
in order, like the grain, to rise again.

But as I stride along the rustling path
and hear the crowd of dying mortals sing,
people as dumb as I sing out his praise:
"O Lord, your blood cries out forever,
my grace fails never, my grace fails never."

Then I am not uneasy with my God.
Then he is close to me, and then I know
that he looks at me from his cup of woe.
Then I can eat his mercy-bread;
then I can live since he was dead.

Thomas

If God existed, he would join us here,
take up our human lot, both yours and mine,
if he could be our bread, or were our wine,
or be the voice which makes our shame appear,

if he could be the green soul deep inside,
the wing which touched the beating of our heart,
the light by which our life got its new start,
or knew our pain, the desert of our pride.

He passes by the stars — a gleam of mist —
a breath of light that's unapproachable.
He is so holy, he does not exist

if I can't really touch him with this hand,
or kiss him with this mouth, with my own face
devour him, burning up in his embrace.

Until He Comes

Until he comes, things will go on this way:
each morning hear the weather and the news,
open the blinds, watch the gray light of day
turn night's deep blackness into morning blue.

A sunlit breakfast starting out each morning,
then into town, tires singing everywhere
along the edges of your little worries;
in the evening news the big ones will appear.

So things repeat themselves from day to day:
familial love around the homey hearth,
children and problems, all the fear that looms.

And finally with your last breath to pay
the fever bills of life; deep in the earth
waiting and listening until he comes.

Communion

We sat around the holy bread and wine,
each by himself, cool strangers in a line
and listened how the breaking raindrops spread
in loud and rushing sheets above our head.
They clattered on the roof, they swept in rolls
and formed strange pools of wonder in our souls.
It felt like the great flood in Noah's ark;
the pastor's voice seemed drowned out in the dark,
but still the grand old words could all be heard:
they blended with that overwhelming word
that kept on beating at the window panes.
We even ventured then to sing a hymn
in which God's goodness and his balm for sin
as if by nature rhymed in with the rain.
And gradually the words became more true
so that we knew God and each other, too.
In God's own language, trembling, we were able
to celebrate communion at his table.

Farmers' Supper

Securely rooted in their earthiness,
unruly, crude, like animals in a stable,
they sit together at the holy table,
these Swedish farmers, Jesus at the head.

Not the trite Savior, sweet, conventional,
the friend of children, walking through the land
with kindly eyes which always understand
and show that he has come to love us all.

No, a rough farmer, totally like them,
who, hand to hand, serves out the bread to all.
If these rough men should burst from off the wall,
a farm rebellion surely would begin.

The Lord's Supper

O God, who perished sinless,
harvest of wine and bread,
you multiplied forever
our life by your dear death.
How wonderful the manner
in which you now appear:
our food, and yet you feed us
as we are seated here.

City View

Serene on this soft autumn day
the town stands dressed in pearly gray.

Spread out along the river's shelf
so stately, drawn within herself,

so proud, with towers holding hands,
a dream of greatness, there she stands.

While I am gazing at that land,
so foreign, yet so close at hand,

a small Dutch city, typical,
and radiantly beautiful,

a string of geese glides into sight,
forming a line, unbroken, white.

Where to and why? Does no one know,
still liberators, where you go

in one straight line? To free the town?
To underline its stern renown?

When that calm scene fades out of sight,
erased by the dark hand of night,

I'll hear their answer from the sky
as crying through the night they fly.

Ice-skating

Over circles winterlight,
glorious streaks of golden hue,
off I skate, god in a poem,
on my snow-white winged shoes.

Every statement that I ride
leads me, leads me through the wind
till I cut the distant line
where the evening-red begins.

Deep within the glassy ice
silent shadows, dark as lead,
flecked with black in every part,

show me mirrored great and gray,
on my head the snow of death,
golden wings upon my heart.

After Ice-skating

Farewell, my ice-skates, butterflies on ice,
footwear as light as any god has worn,
wings like the ones on Hermes' sweeping feet.
He glides, a bird, across the shining air,
appearing, disappearing where he wills.

Farewell, farewell, I turn with wooden feet
over the hardened earth toward home, alas,
a child of death, a small, stiff-walking man,
a Hollander, quite satisfied to sleep

and dream tonight that on swift-flying feet
I sweep along the heavens like a star,
one moment still a god, and then no more.

Fishers

As if this dark horizon brings
beginnings, not the end of things,
the west extends far out of sight
suffused by a relentless light,
as if beyond that burning strand
lay a forbidden, holy land
that spreads its shadows through the air
to sharpen all the contrasts there,
dividing light from dark once more.

So starts anew the endless war
where cosmic good and evil fight,
and in the silver mirror-light
I see in black-etched silhouette
the fishers of Gennasaret.

Praise God

Praise God, who blesses all that lives;
though heaven is his sphere,
he wants to make his home with us —
so far, but still so near.

Praise God, who steers his ship, the church,
he steers it toward the dawn.
He is the heartbeat of our work,
he leads us on and on.

Praise God, whose finger is for us
a tower in our time,
that points creation up to heaven,
eternal and sublime.

Praise God, because he speaks our tongue,
he makes our praise his throne,
in word, in water, bread, and wine
invites us to his home.

Praise God, who bids us eat with him —
our bridegroom, we the bride.
I praise you for my life, dear God,
O, keep me at your side.

Pentecost

As by the Word and Spirit
the world began,
so Pentecost renewed it
for every man.
Just as in every language
it then was heard,
forever it will echo:
God's holy word.

From every church we gather
around you, Lord.
In all our earthly dreaming
you write your word,
O God, who from the heavens
comes down to be
a light for every people
eternally.

City Hall

The proud old house beside the still canal
when it awakens after night's retreat,
is greeted by its image in the stream
as if a dog were lying at its feet.

After the dream of night, a world confused,
the whirling current and the clanking keel,
the daylight brings this image back again,
a mirror-image there, engraved in steel.

Praise be to God, the sun still rises free;
each day escapes the shadow night has cast.
He opens up his daybook, and there stands
this perfect steel-engraving from the past.

An image new as when the world began,
with all the pain of night now washed away,
just as I've always wished that it could be.
I call my dog and walk into the day.

IC
XC

Byzantium Poems

I. Aya Sophia

The moon is standing like a Byzantine coin
above the silver sea of Marmora.
What Christ once granted Caesar as his own
belongs to Caesar; now he leaves it here

where from deep darkness, like a grazing bull,
Aya Sophia's dome looms up on high,
the mother church, the holy middlepoint,
chastened and pure, the crown of Calvary.

The golden God, once banned and covered up,
has risen from the grave of centuries
and in his temple now holds open court:
now Caesar falls before him on his knees.
Yes, even we, in our own godless day,
observe with awe his gentle majesty.

II. Labyrinth

Through all the layers of the labyrinth
winding beneath the dome of the universe,
which rises, the prime number of the world,
the point that holds together the whole earth,
the logos point at which the world begins,
with which it did begin before the fall,
so that it seems to hover over all
the earth below — I seek, but cannot find
in all these layers, what I have in mind.

The meaning of all things is what I seek,
the heart, the secret equilibrium,
the focal point, the wisdom still to come.

At last I find it on the gallery:
it is a God, aglow with majesty,
a man, just as I am; he looks at me.

III. Half Raised

The old mosaic on the wall,
two meters off, across from me,
shows a mild man in purple, gold,
and azure, in the gallery.

Out of the grave of plasterwork
which buried him for centuries,
now half his body has arisen
in this great church for all to see.

With changeless faithfulness and peace,
with true angelic patience, he
blesses the crowds that walk below

with thoughtful kindness, for he dreams
that with the wisdom of his will
the whole world soon will overflow.

IV. Even If . . .

Even if they folded you, immortal God,
as they would strip a flag from off its pole
and lay you in the furrows of the earth
and seal you with the firmest lock they know,

you are yourself, triumphantly you bear
through the dark night your banner with the cross
and carry all your children to their home;
you are yourself, pursue your own good cause.

Over and over buried by mankind,
buried just as you were behind this wall,
you sleep three days or even centuries,

but every time you rise and lift your hand
and hold the book and sound your holy call:
I am the First, I am the Last always.

V. Resurrection

As if he rose out of the grave!
Mankind is his real tomb;
a gray and tragic wave of fear
and love proclaims his doom.

We treat him as a lifeless corpse —
as dead as he can be —
and overwhelm him with a flood
of dark ferocity.

He is as golden as the heavens,
as dark as any night.
And when he lifts his hand to bless,
we kill him at the sight.

But after centuries of death
he blesses us once more.
And we — surprised and wondering —
acknowledge him, the Lord.

inri

Finale

Dogmatics does not teach this anywhere,
unless perhaps in some good book of hymns,
that all the deepest things for which we long
must be fulfilled in music and in song;

and that the judge on that great day of days,
of which the poets wrote throughout the years,
will not speak wrath and judgment to our ears
but give the sign for singing, both hands raised;

and that the angels then will stand in rings,
each playing his own instrument — *en suite* —
and all the holy saints will rise to sing,
watching the great conductor give the beat.

That beat strikes up the music of the spheres —
he motions it with both hands lifted high.
Enthroned in might and splendor he appears,
seated on rainbow arches in the sky.

Notes on the Photographs

page 2 The Lek River, with a view of the village of Revenswaay, Holland

6 Famous fourteenth-century bridge over the river Lot at Cahors, a medieval village in France

12 Grave monument in the village of Katwijk aan den Rijn, Holland, by the seventeenth-century Dutch master of Baroque sculpture, Rombout Verhulst

18 Detail from a baptismal font in Sillenstede, Oost-Friesland, Holland, in which Christ's rescue of Jonah symbolizes the harrowing of hell

22 Sculpture of a famous sixteenth-century French military commander

26 Fresco in the church in Tingsted, a village on the island of Falster, Denmark

30 Lavastone in Les Baux, an old ruined town near Arles, France, famous for its intricate rock formations

34 Grave monument in the church of St. Oswald in the village of Malpas, Chester, England

40 Eighteenth-century folk art fresco in an old Romanesque church in the village of Väversunda in the province of East Gothland, Sweden

44 The city of Kampen along the shore of the Ijssel River in the province of Overijssel, Holland

48 Fishers near the village of Teignmouth in Devonshire, England

52 The old city hall in the small provincial town of Franeker in Friesland, Holland

54 The Half-Raised Christ, a mosaic depicting the glorification of Christ, located on the south balcony of the Aya Sophia in Istanbul; it was plastered over in the fifteenth century by the Turks and then partially uncovered in 1918

60 Fresco in a burial chapel built by a musical Lutheran family in 1560 in Rynkeby, near Odense, Denmark, which depicts Christ conducting thirty-two angels playing a variety of musical instruments